Jo Draper has been researching on Dorset for thirty years. She was Editor of the *Proceedings of the Dorset Natural History & Archaeological Society* for fifteen years, and has written several books on the county including *Dorset: the Complete Guide*, *Dorset Food* and three books on Dorchester. With John Fowles she wrote *Thomas Hardy's England*. She lives in Dorchester with her husband, with whom she wrote *Walking Dorset History*.

Following page
Blandford in 1948. The town was totally rebuilt in the 1730s after a disastrous fire. The little 'temple' at the east end of the Market Place is the monument to the fire, whilst the building in the background, facing the church, was originally the house of John Bastard, one of the two brothers responsible for much of the Georgian town.

THE GEORGIANS

JO DRAPER

THE DOVECOTE PRESS

The almshouses in East Street, Wareham, originally
founded by John Streche (died 1418), and rebuilt
in classical style in 1741.

First published in 1998 by The Dovecote Press Ltd
Stanbridge, Wimborne, Dorset BH21 4JD

ISBN 1 874336 54 7

© Jo Draper 1998

Jo Draper has asserted her rights under the Copyright, Designs
and Patents Act 1988 to be identified as author of this work

Series designed by Humphrey Stone

Typeset in Sabon by The Typesetting Bureau
Wimborne, Dorset
Printed and bound by Baskerville Press, Salisbury, Wiltshire

A CIP catalogue record for this book is available
from the British Library

1 3 5 7 9 8 6 4 2

CONTENTS

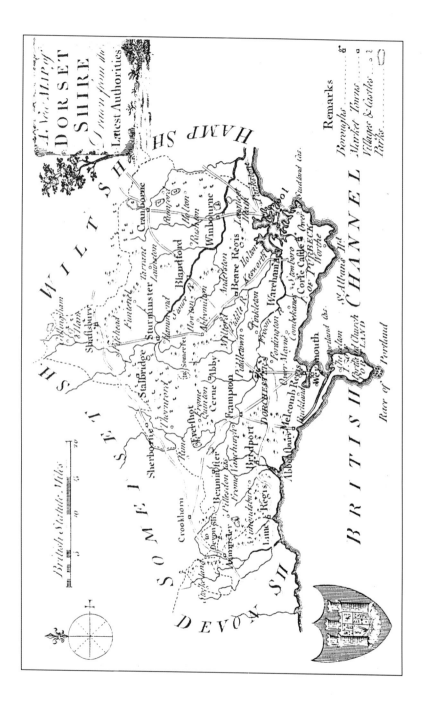

THE LAND OF DORSET

Dorset was much admired by Georgian visitors: Benjamin Martin, who described the whole country in his *Natural History of England* (1759) declared that, in Dorset 'there is no Want of any Thing, that is necessary for the Maintenance and Support of Man; since both Sea and Land seem to vie with each other, and strive which shall indulge his Appetite most, and yield him the greatest Abundance. To all this we must add, that its fine Beer and Ale are universally admired, and by some preferred before the Wines of *France*'. Martin found it no great wonder that 'such a Number of Families, even of high Distinction, make it their favourite Place of Abode; and that notwithstanding its Capital is above one hundred miles from *London*, its Inhabitants are as gay and polite, as those in our Metropolitan City.'

Since Georgian Dorset was, like almost all of England then, an agricultural county, most of the population was employed in farming, and the majority were small farmers or labourers, few of whom were likely to be as 'gay and polite' as London society. Like most contemporary writers, Martin was only concerned with the aristocracy and gentry, a tiny minority of Dorset's inhabitants.

The county itself divided into three very different parts, depending on the geology. The high chalk downland was open and unfenced, and many eighteenth century writers comment on the fineness of the turf it produced, and the high quality of the mutton from the sheep who grazed it. The downs were regarded as valuable because they fed

'A New Map of Dorsetshire, 1784'. Corfe Castle is included amongst the seven boroughs because it had the right to send MPs to Parliament. The little staked enclosures are parks or chases for hunting. The map misses out most of the roads, and even omits some of the turnpikes, like the Salisbury-Blandford turnpike which by-passed Cranborne. North of Cerne Abbas (Abby on the map) is a detached part of Somerset. The arms are those of the town of Dorchester.

An engraving of Upwey House from Hutchins *History of Dorset*, (1774). In the foreground a man, boy and two horses are ploughing arable land. In the background rise the bare chalk hills. The manor house is seventeenth century, but neat Georgian stables have been added, and on the improbably steep hill to the right is a little Georgian gazebo.

so many sheep, but as landscape they were not admired, being too bleak and open for Georgian taste. William Maton (1797) is typical - the chalk gives 'an open, unornamented prospect'.

The clay vales with their deep rich soils, neat fences, hedges, and orchards made a much more domestic countryside and fitted well with ideas of a prosperous and therefore attractive landscape.

The heathlands, which then stretched all across south-east Dorset, were hated. Barren, dreary waste is the usual Georgian verdict, and they thought improvement was greatly needed. Until the Romantic movement later in the eighteenth century, landscape was judged for its usefulness and profit, not for its picturesque qualities.

The farming of the three regions was very different. On the chalk the high parts were the open downs, inhabited only by shepherds and their flocks. The farms and villages were down in the valleys along with the arable fields. The fertility of the arable was maintained by folding the sheep across them, so that their manure was spread on the fields. The sheep were tightly folded in hurdled enclosures which were gradually moved across the fields. This was vital to corn growing on the thin chalk soil: without them the arable would soon have become infertile. Because of this sheep were known as 'walking dung carts' or 'the golden hoof'.

Water meadows played an important role in feeding the sheep early in the year, when grass was scarce. Watering was particularly suited to chalkland valleys, and thousands of acres of water meadows were constructed in Dorset from the seventeenth century onwards. Elaborate systems of weirs, hatches and channels fed a thin sheet of moving water over the field, which protected it from frost and kept it warm. The silt from the water also enriched the ground, so that good crops of early grass were produced. The sheep manure from this rich grass was particularly prized, and came at just the right time to fertilise land which was to be used for spring sowing.

This chalkland farming system of the eighteenth century was an integrated whole, with the sheep and grasslands together supplying the manure which maintained corn production.

Then, as now, the Blackmore Vale and the vales of west Dorset

Looking from Poundbury to Dorchester in 1796, a water-colour by J. W. Upham. The pattern of channels which fed water over the water-meadows is clear on the left. The lady and gentleman sensibly walk with their dog on the fine dry chalkland turf of Poundbury, and the town of Dorchester is enclosed in trees background right. The building in the centre is a mill.

were grazing country, supporting large herds of cattle. Small areas of arable were mostly used to grow roots and so on for cattle feed, but corn had to be grown for rotation. Many of the cattle were being fattened for the meat market, but the area also had lots of small dairy farms. These produced for sale not milk, but butter and cheese. Milk sales at any distance were impossible before fast transport, but cheese and butter were more durable. All agricultural writers comment on the unusual letting arrangement for Dorset dairies: the landowner or farmer supplied the dairyman with the cows and their keep, while the dairyman paid a rent based on the number of cows. The skimmed milk and by-products from cheese-making (whey etc.) were usually fed to pigs, and much cider was also made from the many orchards which flourished in the vales.

The heathlands were described by Hutchins in 1774 as 'the most barren part of the county; and nature, who has in other parts

Urless Farm, Corscombe in 1747, in a neat, productive landscape.
Sheep are scattered over the distant hills.

The Blackmore Vale: cattle grazing the meadows near Fifehead Magdalen.

distributed her beauties with so liberal a hand, seems here, by way of
contrast, to exhibit a view of all others the most dreary and unpleas-
ing.' He admitted that it supplied the inhabitants with fuel (peat and
furze) and provided grazing for a few beasts, but he admired only the
improving landowners who had managed to tame some of it into
farmland. 'These appear as gardens in midst of a desert.' Planting firs
on the heathland had just begun in the later eighteenth century.

The reclaimed heathland was the most obvious example of the
improvers' energy, but many aspects of agriculture were gradually
refined. Progress was steady rather than spectacular: manuring was
improved, and the use of chalk for marling spread. More systematic
breeding of animals improved cattle, sheep, pigs and horses, and
new crops like turnips and 'artificial' (especially sown rather than
natural) grasses started to be grown. Farmers kept more records, and
gradually agriculture became more scientific.

The land of Dorset was not owned by those who farmed it. Much
of the county belonged to gentry families, and most of the farmers
were their tenants. The Strangways (the Earls of Ilchester), the Dig-
bys of Sherborne; the Ashley-Coopers (the Earls of Shaftesbury), the
Sturts of Crichel, the Bankes and so on all held huge estates in the
county. Milton Abbas, held by the Damer family, was at the centre of
an estate of 8,600 acres covering most of four parishes.

TOWNS, PORTS AND VILLAGES

The basic pattern of the county was much as today, but with most of the settlements (especially the towns) on a very much smaller scale. The eleven inland towns and four ports in the county were already old settlements, but Bournemouth did not yet exist. Dorset also had about 270 villages, of which perhaps thirteen were large and had some claim to be towns. A few medieval villages had died out.

THE TOWNS

The inland towns were all small and clearly defined. None were large enough to straggle into the countryside with suburbs. Dorchester, the county town, was much the same size as the four other largest inland ones - Sherborne Shaftesbury, Wimborne and Bridport. These five had between 3,000-3,500 inhabitants in 1801, the first census. Six other towns had populations ranging from 1,500-2,500: Blandford, Wareham, Sturminster Newton, Gillingham, Beaminster and Cranborne. Cranborne was described by Dr Richard Pococke in 1754 as 'a poor small town, consisting chiefly of farmers, a few shops, and public houses', and most of the other small towns would have been similar.

Although these towns only had the population of one of today's larger villages, there were properly urban. They had a market, shops, banks, specialised craftsmen (like silversmiths), the lawyers and physicians needed to service a large rural area, and they were the centre for transport of people and goods. Many had industries, like cloth-making at Dorchester or rope manufacture at Bridport, and most of the secondary schools were urban. The towns were commercial and social centres, and provided the markets needed to sell agricultural produce.

The appearance of most of the towns was altered enormously in

Blandford market place in 1948, with the Town Hall on the left.

the eighteenth century. Taller classical buildings with bigger sash
windows replaced the earlier houses. Brick was used much more
frequently, and many of the older buildings which survived, did so
behind a new façade. Blandford is the most extreme example: after a
bad fire in 1731 virtually the whole town was rebuilt. It all survives
today, giving a complete picture of a Georgian market town.

The centre of Blandford is the market place, enlarged in the new
post-fire town, surrounded by rather plain, regular brick houses. The
Town Hall in the middle of the market place is distinguished by
being built of stone, as is the church, tucked away off one side of the
market place. Three large inns are of similar pattern to the houses.

The centre of the town provided homes, workshops and shops for
craftsmen and shop-keepers. The buildings in the centre are terraced,
producing a continuous street frontage. Set just back from the centre are large detached houses, mostly of brick, but sometimes with
stone door and window surrounds. These were the houses of the
gentry. On side streets and the outer reaches of the main roads,

Above Eastway House, Blandford, built in about 1735, with an elaborate
doorway and urns on the roof added in about 1750. This house is
typical of the highest quality Georgian town buildings, with its handsome
and well-proportioned street frontage, and inside some elaborate
plasterwork. The 1930s photograph shows the original iron railings
and gate, since replaced.

Opposite page Bridport Town Hall, built in 1785-6, with the clock and
cupola added in about 1805. The open ground floor was used for markets.

Looking into Blandford market place in August 1794, from a drawing by Thomas Baskerfield. The Town Hall is in the middle of the market, with the church beyond. Many of the town centre houses have ground floor shops.

Part of the Market at Weymouth in 1790, by John Nixon. These
seventeenth century houses and the old Guildhall survived until 1837
– most Georgian towns had many earlier buildings, old and low
by contrast with the new houses.

smaller houses and cottages were built for artisans and labourers.

Blandford is unusual because virtually the whole town was rebuilt,
but the same sort of pattern (with the intermixing of older buildings) would have been found in all the towns, although the others
preserved their medieval churches. Many town halls were replaced
by larger, more classical ones during the Georgian period: Bridport
has a particularly fine brick one of 1785 right in the middle of the
town. At Bridport, as with most of the Dorset town halls, the lower
part doubled up as a market hall.

The weekly markets held in the towns were where many of the
farming products were sold. Horses, cattle and sheep were also
traded at the annual fairs, but corn, butter, cheese and potatoes were
the weekly staples of the market. Country people came into town to
buy as well to sell, so the markets also sold cloth, imported
groceries and other luxuries, besides agricultural equipment, seeds,
and so on.

Even though it was the county town, Dorchester was no larger than the other inland towns. Unlike Blandford, it was a mixture of old and new. All three of its churches were medieval, and many low seventeenth century stone or timber-framed houses survived to contrast with the new taller brick town houses. When Daniel Defoe visited in the 1720s he found 'the streets broad, but the buildings old and low.' Several fires and the desire for modern houses cleared the way for patchy rebuilding, so that by the end of the century the town had a mixture of housing, a new classical town hall and shire hall and a couple of small but equally classical non-conformist chapels. Dr Richard Pococke in 1754 defined the economy of Dorchester: 'They have a manufacture of linsey woolsey [a type of cloth], they make malt, and are famous for beer, but the chief support of the town is the thoroughfare to Exeter, and the nobility and gentry who live near it'. Dorchester's position as a junction on several coach routes was very important.

Defoe was impressed by Dorchester in the early eighteenth century: 'a pleasant agreeable town to live in, where I thought the people seemed less divided into factions and parties, than in other places. Here I saw the Church of England clergyman, and the dissenting minister drinking tea together, and conversing with civility and good neighbourhood . . . there is good company and a good deal of it; and

A late eighteenth century Dorchester seedman's card. The classical decorations include swags of roses.

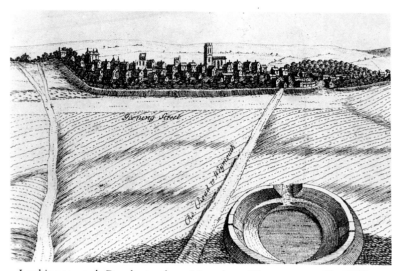

Looking towards Dorchester from Maumbury Rings, engraved by William Stukely, 1723. The abrupt edge of the town is clear, with open fields running right up to the bank, all that was left of the Roman defences.

a man that coveted a retreat in this world might as agreeably spend his time, and as well in Dorchester, as in any town I know in England.'

He was gratified to find that 'the ladies here do not want the help of assemblies to assist in match-making; or half-pay officers to run away with their daughters.' He would have been sorry to know how soon assembly rooms were established in all the Dorset towns - by the end of the century everywhere had at least a large room attached to the principal inn where balls, dances and meetings for playing cards could be held.

THE PORTS AND THE SEA

At the time of the first census in 1801, Poole was the largest town in the county, with 4,800 inhabitants. The largest inland towns had only 3,000 people. Weymouth (with its twin Melcombe Regis) had 3,600 inhabitants, but the other two ports were much smaller - Lyme Regis and Swanage had only 1,400 people each.

Poole in the late eighteenth century, with a forest of ship's masts. The ships seem tiny, but they crossed the Atlantic regularly. The coastal trading ships were slightly smaller, and have been compared to modern lorries as their loads were similar.

Apart from Lyme with its artificial harbour (the Cobb), the placing of the ports was fixed by the position of natural harbours. Poole was at the head of the largest natural harbour in the world, and Weymouth was also well sited at the mouth of a river.

In the eighteenth century these long-established ports had a mixture of trading routes. Smaller ships moved many types of goods along the coast, and carried goods and passengers to London. Swanage specialised in exporting the stone quarried nearby, and Weymouth with Portland similarly moved the Portland stone.

Daniel Defoe in the 1720s thought Poole 'a considerable sea-port, and indeed the most considerable in all this part of England ...

especially here were a great number of ships fitted out every year to the Newfoundland fishing, in which the Pool men were said to have been particularly successful for many years past.'

The Newfoundland trade was a complex one. Ships from Poole (and Weymouth) took salt and general supplies out to Newfoundland, fished for cod which was salted, returned to the Mediterranean to sell the fish, finally coming back to England with wine, raisins, olive oil and other Mediterranean produce. The complete trip took over six months, leaving England usually in March. It was risky: crossing the Atlantic in small ships was much more dangerous than coastal trading. If all went well, the Newfoundland trade was very profitable, and several Poole families made fortunes from it.

All the ports built ships as well as sailing them. Even tiny coastal settlements like West Bay (then called Bridport Harbour) had their shipyards.

Much of Dorset's coast was treacherous, and huge quantities of shipping used the route up the English Channel. Portland and Chesil were particularly feared because of their difficult tides and the strong currents off Portland Bill. Wrecks were common, and sometimes even contrived, by luring ships onto rocks with false lights. Portlanders were particularly bold in robbing wrecked ships. When a Dutch vessel was driven ashore in 1748 near Fleet, 'the men of Portland, Wyke and Waymouth, formed themselves into a body with colours [i.e. like an army] to secure the goods that floated along the coast . . . the Captain [of the ship] was obliged to retire' from the fray. The weather was so cold, that some of the looters perished on the beach. For ten days there was anarchy: 'the shore was a scene of unheard-of riot, violence, and barbarity.' It was the richest wreck ever seen on these coasts because it was carrying quantities of gold. In this case the crew all survived, but sometimes drowning or injured men were ignored by the wreckers in their lust for goods.

Serious advice and fair warning was the title of a sermon preached at Fleet in 1754 by a local rector who had been an eye-witness of several local wrecks. He chastised his flock for being 'intent only on plunder, and so barbarous and inhuman, as to take advantage of the distresses of those unhappy sufferers' who were shipwrecked. He compared their actions to helping a neighbour put out a fire in his barn, and then robbing the barn straightaway afterwards.

Some of those involved in wrecking were certainly also smugglers. In the eighteenth century contraband trade in the many types of goods which carried heavy duties was widespread throughout the county. Brandy and tea were the staples, but gin, lace and even chocolate were also traded. The romantic picture of picturesque free-traders, loved by everyone for their gentleness and co-opera-tion, is untrue. Smuggling was simply a business, and by the later eighteenth century, big business. Large gangs carried the smuggled goods from the shore to distribution points inland, and terrified the countryside by their violence.

The Preventative Officers and Revenue men who were supposed to catch the smugglers were often in league with them. The school-master at Christchurch, from his eyrie on top of the priory church remembered seeing 'A procession of twenty or thirty wagons loaded with kegs of spirits, an armed man sitting at the front and tail of each, surrounded by a troop of two or three hundred horsemen, every one carrying on his enormous saddle from two to four tubs of spirits' winding along the deserted shore near Hengistbury. 'The Revenue troop, were it is true, present, but with no other views and intentions than those of perfect peace. A flood of homely jokes were poured upon them by the passing ruffians' but the Revenue men were happy as they were taking some of the kegs of spirits as a toll, to sell for themselves.

Although the gangs were frightening when moving around with their hauls, most people were sympathetic because they bought tea and spirits from the smugglers. A gravestone to Robert Trotman, who was killed while smuggling near Poole in 1765 includes:

> *A little Tea, one leaf I did not steal*
> *For Guiltless Blood shed I to GOD appeal*
> *Put Tea in one scale human blood in t'other*
> *And think what 'tis to slay thy harmless brother*

Revenue men were also killed. The violence and risk of losing a cargo was made up for by the great profits a successful run brought.

Two of Dorset's ports developed in Georgian times into seabathing resorts, part of a national trend away from the old inland spas with their medicinal waters. Weymouth and Lyme Regis started attracting visitors from the 1750s, but reached the peak of fashion later in the century. Weymouth's wide sheltered bay and fine sands were perfect for bathing, and like Lyme, the surrounding scenery was also suitably picturesque.

A medical treatise on sea-bathing, with especial reference to Weymouth, was published by a Dr Crane, who advised talking the dip early in the morning, since 'To Bathe late in the Day, (more especially in hot Weather) will occasion great Depression of Spirits'. A temporary depression or 'A Chilliness or Shivering for a Time' was induced by 'staying imprudently too long in the Water'. Successful bathers would 'find their Spirits exhilarated, and feel an universal Glow thow the System.'

A late eighteenth century *Guide* describes the three Inns, one with 'A Coffee-Room, supplied with the London and County Papers and the Libraries, Shops of Millinery, Mercery &c, as well as Toy Shops, Music and Print Shops'. An Assembly Room for evening entertainments and a theatre completed the resort, which gained the accolade of Royal patronage from 1789. George III, with some of his large family, made fourteen summer or autumn visits between 1789-1805.

An account of a visit to Weymouth in 1804 describes the varied effects the Royal visitors had on the town. Because the Royal party arose at 5 a.m. to be out by 6, Weymouth shops opened at 5.30 a.m. to be ready for the early morning rush, 'for by six the streets were as thronged with all the fashionables at court, and also by those who were anxious to be thought so, as Regent Street [London].' The King dined at three, and was on the Esplanade at six in the evening, a routine everyone else felt obliged to follow.

Opposite page top George III bathing at Weymouth. Georgians did not simply leap into the sea and frolic (although local children certainly did). Bathing was a serious medicinal occasion. The machine was pulled out into reasonably deep water by a horse. One, or even two, attendants helped (or if necessary pushed) the bather into the water for a specified period of immersion. Women bathers wore special bathing clothing, men rather less. *Opposite page bottom* The improved bathing machine built for George III to use at Weymouth in 1791. Most bathing machines had a hood (seen on the left) which could be pulled down to give the bather privacy.

'Farmer George', King George III walking on Weymouth Esplanade in 1797.
His homeliness is emphasised in this cartoon: George III was domestic
and not glamorous. Every time he left his house crowds like this,
even at six in the morning, surrounded him.

The Royal visits made Weymouth fashionable, but it was never so
stylish as its rival Brighton, where George III's son held sway. The
Royal visits were respectable family parties, with seaborne excur-
sions, bathing, gentle touring and visits to Portland.

Not everyone approved of Weymouth (or indeed the other
resorts). The crotchety Hon John Byng (later Viscount Torrington)
visited Weymouth in August 1782, and complained continually. 'At
these places there is ever an abundance of the fair-sex, being so well
adapted for the elder ladies to get cards and company, and for the
misses to procure flattery, lovers, and sometimes husbands. That the
infirm, and the upstarts, should resort to these fishing holes, may
perhaps be accounted for; but that the healthy owners of parks, good
houses and good beds, should quit them for confinement, dirt, and
misery, appears to me to be downright madness.' Byng was
particularly sensitive about beds, as he had suffered some really bad
ones on the journey down. He was visiting his wife and three female
friends in Weymouth who were 'all expecting to drown their nervous
fears, and hysterical wanderings, in the sea, assisted by the use of

genteel dancing with soft speeches from beaus, and the indulgence of polite conversation'. Soft speeches and polite conversation from Mr Byng seems a bit unlikely: he disliked Weymouth, complained about his company, and found the price of provisions much too high.

VILLAGES AND FARMS

At the 1801 census Dorset had about 270 villages, thirteen of which had populations of around 1,000 and probably regarded themselves as small towns. Twenty-two more had populations ranged from 500-800, but by far the greatest majority varied from fifty to three hundred people. The one hundred and sixty villages in this range of population showed a huge variation from hamlets like Chilcombe (23 people) to thriving centres like West Lulworth or Pimperne.

The settlements varied a great deal, but Dorset has a model Georgian village which reflects what landowners thought the ideal one should be. In 1780 the owner of the small town of Milton Abbas

Gloucester Lodge, Weymouth, built in 1780 for the Duke of Gloucester, a younger brother of George III, but used by the King during his visits to Weymouth. The good proportions and plain windows are typical of Georgian architecture. From a watercolour by J.W. Upham, 1802.

The new village of 1780 at Milton Abbas. The large cottages were originally semi-detached pairs. Their regularity and setting, along with the big trees between each house, made them very picturesque.

decided to have it demolished because it was too close to his mansion. He replaced it by a much smaller village, tucked into a valley a good distance from the big house.

Milton Abbas had new cottages, mill, church and a vicarage, along with seventeenth century almshouses moved from the old town. The mill was brick, but the large vicarage was of cob like the cottages. Stone was reserved for the church. Milton Abbas had all the buildings necessary for a village: cottages for the labourers; farmhouses for the farmers, a typically large vicarage; an inn (which in this case also catered for travellers coming to see the big house); and a mill to grind the corn. The almshouse for the aged was a bonus which few villages enjoyed. A brewery also survived the move from town to village.

Pairs of thatched cottages built of cob were the standard building - Fanny Burney saw them in 1791 and complained that 'every house

The Vicarage at Milton Abbas, rebuilt about 1780, was constructed of cob, like the cottages, but is much larger and has big sash windows and an elaborate doorway.

was square and meant to resemble a gentleman's abode: a very miserable mistake . . . for the sight of the common people, and of the poor, labouring or strolling in and about these dwellings, made them appear rather to be reduced from better days than flourishing in a primitive or natural state.'

Burney also complained of the 'comic, irregular, odd, old houses' in Dorchester, so it is difficult to see what she thought was ideal, although she did think both Charmouth and Chideock villages 'the very prettiest I ever did see', so she must have preferred stone to timber framing or cob.

The big house at Milton Abbas was larger and richer than those found in most Dorset parishes, but virtually every village had one. The mansion was usually set apart from the cottages so that those who lived in them could enjoy gardens, grounds and views.

All the other villages of Dorset were much more irregular than

A cottage-like farmhouse at Morden dating from the late eighteenth century, with its small barn beyond, contrasts with the much more middle-class farmhouse from Lytchett Minster. Both are brick, and neither represent extremes – there were much smaller and much larger farmhouses in the county.

Milton Abbas. Many cottages were built in the eighteenth century, but earlier ones were still in use. The cottages of the period were much more varied than those which still survive, because only the larger and better-built cottages have withstood three hundred years' wear and tear.

Thatch was still the usual roofing material, except in Purbeck where stone slates were used for the more expensive buildings. Cottages were one room deep, which is what gives them their characteristic long façades.

FARMS AND FARMHOUSES

Eighteenth century farmhouses range from buildings just like the cottages inhabited by the labourers up to large houses, which became more common as farms increased in size. John Claridge described the average farm in 1798 as 'A small low house of stone, and covered with slate, situate in a bottom' (i.e. in the valley). He thought that Dorset farmers had fewer farm buildings than the rest of the country, only needing two barns (one small) a stable, cow-house, and cart-house. A dairyman's house would be needed if the dairy were separately let. 'The farmer's usual method is to stack his hay on the ground, where he is likely to fodder [i.e. feed the animals] in the winter, and his corn on stone rick staddles, in a yard adjoining to the buildings.'

Earlier farmhouses were often actually part of the farmyard, but later in the Georgian period the larger farmhouses were set at a little distance, showing the separation of the farmer from direct involvement with the stock, and his growing social status. In the older farms, master and men had eaten together at the same table: in the new large houses the farmers were becoming middle class or even lower gentry. Their daughters were learning to play the piano, rather than milking the cows; and their sons were being educated like gentlemen rather than ploughing the fields.

Cheaper local imitation of stylish London furniture was popular with these newly middle class farmers, and much of the 'country Georgian' furniture surviving today started life in a farmhouse.

MANSIONS AND MANOR HOUSES

The larger houses built in Georgian Dorset range from the mansions of the aristocracy down to handsome rectories and farmhouses.

As well as the model village, Milton Abbas has one of the largest Georgian mansions in the county. It was built in a slightly Gothic style to match the surviving late medieval hall of the abbey, whereas most houses were classical, but it shows all the features required from a large Georgian house. Privacy was important - the old town of Milton Abbas, adjacent to the house was cleared away, and re-placed by a carefully constructed landscape to provide a suitable setting. An artificial lake was made, and woods planted to ornament the view. The house was separated from the village and farms which supported it, whereas earlier it would not have shunned them.

The poet Alexander Pope poked fun at the huge size of gardens and grounds - 'His pond an Ocean, his parterre a Down', and hoped:

> *Another Age shall see the golden Ear*
> *Imbrown the Slope, and nod on the Parterre,*
> *Deep Harvests bury all his pride has plann'd,*
> *And laughing Ceres re-assume the land.*

The local poet William Holloway regretted the change because of the effect on smaller farmers:

> *Where now the park extends, and useless deer*
> *Along the solitary glades appear,*
> *Rich corn-fields wav'd, in spacious prospect spread,*
> *Nor felt one villager the want of bread.*

The mansion at Milton Abbas, with the medieval abbey church beside it. The old town was to the right of the abbey: the new village is invisibly tucked into a valley. The house is set in a created landscape of park and woodland.

In John O'Keefe's *The London Hermit or Rambles in Dorsetshire* (a play of 1793 based on his sojourns in West Lulworth) one of the older gentry characters complains about his neighbour's new gardens: 'the five thousand pounds you laid out upon that clumsy Pantheon yonder, would have built a neat cluster of almshouses, where age and infancy might find an asylum from the pangs of indigence.' He is stating an old-fashioned point of view, that wealth should be used for the good of the lower orders, rather than for display. But his were minority views: most people were impressed by the scale of Milton Abbas.

Hutchins describes the house, 'standing in a truly monastic valley, on a beautiful undulating lawn, surrounded by an amphitheatre of hills, whose summits are crowned with woods planted with great taste by the earl above-mentioned. The drives through the plantations are very varied, and extend more than ten miles, within a ring fence. The park wall is five miles and quarter in length. The approach from Blandford is by two lodges and an iron gate, through an avenue of laurel hedges backed by timber trees. To this entrance a private road was made through fields and woods by the first earl, and the gates kept locked. There is also a deer-park.'

Hutchins seems particularly impressed by the private road, which is kept locked: a good symbol of the domination of the landscape.

The house itself was enormous, but nothing like so large as Eastbury, Dorset's finest Georgian mansion. Eastbury was built by Bubb Dodington, created Baron Melcombe Regis in 1761 just before his death. He was the son of a Weymouth apothecary, and after a very successful (and corrupt) political life (and inheriting a large fortune), built his huge mansion to the design of Vanbrugh from the 1720s. Mrs Philip Powys, visiting in 1760, marvelled at the main front, extending in length 570 ft, of which the main body of the house took up only 144; the rest was arcades and offices. She was impressed by the furnishings, with marble tables 'the housekeeper inform'd us, out of one of the Italian palaces.' Others were shocked by the vulgarity: Richard Cumberland mocked 'the turrets and wings that went I know not where ... and the interior was as proud and splendid as the exterior was bold and imposing. All this was exactly in unison with the taste of the magnificent owner, who had gilt and

An eighteenth century painting of Eastbury, the house designed by
Vanbrugh for Bubb Doddington outside Tarrant Gunville, once
the largest house in Dorset.

Bubb Dodington. Cumberland unkindly wrote, 'his bulk and
corpulence gave full display to a vast expanse of brocade and
embroidery and this, when set off with an enormous
tyeperriwig, and deep-laced ruffles, gave the picture of an
ancient courtier in his gala habit'.

Bryanston House in 1714, showing the old house and its huge formal gardens. These became less fashionable in the late eighteenth century, and were replaced by more natural layouts incorporating clumps of trees and lakes. The house was demolished in 1788 and replaced by a new mansion, designed by James Wyatt, which in turn was demolished and replaced by the existing mansion in 1890.

furnished the apartments with a profusion of finery ... He was rarely seated but under painted ceilings and gilt entablatures ... he slept in a bed encanopied with peacocks feathers... when he passed it was always in a coach drawn by six fat, black, unwieldy horses.' After Dodington's death the house was demolished: it was too large and rich for anyone else.

The poet Alexander Pope derided the ostentation of these houses:

> But Hark! the chiming clocks to dinner call;
> A hundred footsteps scrape the marble hall:
> The rich buffet well-coloured serpents grace,
> And gaping Tritons spew to wash your face.
> Is this a dinner? This a Genial room?
> No, tis a Temple, and a Hetacomb.

The huge mansions of the aristocracy were not numerous, but virtually every village had a manor house (or simply 'big' house) belonging to the local squire. Some were rebuilt in the eighteenth century, but many of the squires continued to live in the sturdy houses their forebears had built in the sixteenth and seventeenth centuries. Living in an old house emphasised the antiquity of the family, but like the churches, the house was likely to be refitted inside. Older buildings were respected, but it was modern

Came House, Winterborne Came, built in 1754 by Sir John Damer, and designed by the Blandford architect, Francis Cartwright. The wing on the right housed the kitchen, and was linked to the main building by a corridor. The other smaller building is probably the stables.

Symondsbury Rectory dwarfing the local cottages, from Hutchins *History of Dorset*, 1796. It was one of the richest livings in the county, and the parsonage was of a size to match. Contemporaries complained that the money spent on rectories should have been spent on churches.

The Rectory, now known as John's House, Spetisbury, was built in 1716 by the rector Dr Charles Sloper, and is one of the earliest of the many large rectories built in Dorset in the eighteenth century. Dr Sloper also paid for the rebuilding of Charlton Marshall church, and left most of his money to charity when he died in 1727. Rectories like these vied with the manor house in size, and reflected the wealth of some rectors. Spetisbury rectory is of fashionable red brick, with a handsome staircase and panelled rooms inside.

architecture which was admired. The county has many examples of Georgian large houses, ranging from the early eighteenth century Chettle to Pennsylvania Castle on Portland, built in 1800.

Rectories could be as large as manor houses. Georgian clergymen were not paid a standard wage - some clergy were paid astonishingly high stipends and others were very poor. Symondsbury was the richest in the county in the mid-eighteenth century at £500 a year, with some tithes as well. Symondsbury rectory was of a size to match the living.

THE CHURCH

The Georgian church, both buildings and people, were deeply disapproved of by the Victorians. Certainly the church was at a low ebb in the eighteenth century, and some of its ministers were ineffective, but the Victorians exaggerated the problem because that made their reforms seem even more effective.

The Victorians disliked Georgian church architecture because it was classical in style rather than medieval, and often replaced it, so only the few complete churches built in the eighteenth century survive, along with a tiny proportion of the Georgian additions and alterations. Much of the money spent on churches during the eighteenth century in Dorset went on maintaining the county's large stock of medieval ones.

Charlton Marshall church was completely rebuilt in 1713, and gives a good idea of an early Georgian church because most of its fittings survive. Externally the church is rather plain and austere, with classical windows and doors, but the fittings are much more elaborate, with big pulpit and reredos, both decorated in a classical style. The emphasis on the pulpit is typical: the preaching of the sermon was the most important part of the service. Originally the church was filled with box pews, with 4-5ft high sides, but the Victorians cut them down to form benches.

The social divisions were preserved even inside the churches: landowners and the gentry had private family pews (which they actually owned) at the front of the church, or even in the chancel. These were often nicely carpeted and cushioned, and had curtains to cut down the draughts. Labourers and other lower people sat at the back on benches, which were sometimes labelled 'For the Poor'. Special seats for the Mayor, or churchwardens were often provided. Even in death there were great differences: the better off were likely to be buried inside the church, and have elaborate monuments erected to them on

The eigthteenth century font at Charlton Marshall shows all the
features that the Victorians disapproved of – light-hearted
classical details like the swags of foliage had no place in a
Victorian church. The neat wooden top with its pineapple
finial is typical of high-quality Georgian woodwork.

the walls. The lower classes were buried outside in the churchyard,
and at best had only a headstone.

Blandford Forum church was rebuilt with the rest of the town after
the great fire of 1731 and has many windows to make the interior
light. Other churches tried to gain the same effect by adding more
windows and whitewashing the walls inside. Hutchins (1815) records

Corscombe church, largely rebuilt in the late eighteenth century: 'a neat building. . .well-pewed, as spruce and neat as white-lime &c can make it.' Bright, neat and spruce were virtues in a Georgian church.

St George Reforne on Portland is a much more sophisticated building than the earlier Georgian churches, with a complicated classical tower, but the most surprising church is St Mary's East Lulworth, the first Catholic church to be built in England since the sixteenth century. The Weld family were given personal permission by George III to build the Catholic church, so long as it looked like a family mausoleum.

Many Georgian fittings were added to medieval churches. Box pews were fitted in virtually every church, and so were tables of commandments (boards with the ten commandments painted on).

Humble Georgian fittings seldom survived the Victorians. This photograph of the church at Gussage St Andrew in 1888 catches it just before 'restoration' removed the simple Georgian box pews. They are a reminder that surviving Georgian woodwork tends to be the high quality work.

St George, Reforne, Portland, built in the mid eighteenth century.
The tower is particularly impressive, with its classical detailing:
the main body of the church looks a bit like a house.

Every church gained memorial tablets which ranged from vast monuments with life-sized figures down to small tablets, often beautifully
lettered. A wooden reredos behind the altar, decorated with classical
pediments and other details sometimes obscured the east window.
Stained glass was no longer made, but occasionally painted glass was
fitted. Plain glass and larger windows was preferred as a light interior
was desired. Black and white stone floors, just like those in the better
houses, were sometimes laid in the chancels. The chancel of the old
church at Bothenhampton and Chalbury church still both preserve a
Georgian style inside because of their fittings, but on a tiny scale.

Galleries were constructed in many churches in Georgian times

The fine wooden reredos at Abbotsbury church dates from 1751. The
capitals and other details are gilded, including the very un-churchy jugs on
the pediment. It completely blocks off the east window.

because the population had increased and more seats were needed for the congregation. The church bands were also usually housed in a gallery at the back of the church. These bands of singers and instrumentalists led the congregational singing and provided all the music for the services. They were usually only a small group, playing

Sherborne Abbey in the 1840s, still with its high Georgian pews. Virtually every church had these enclosed seats, and all were removed (or cut down) by the Victorians. Richard Paget, visiting Sherborne in 1790, complained that the interior of the abbey church was 'vilely choak'd up with Pews'.

stringed instruments (including viols) or wind instruments like clarionets, serpents, and recorders. Hardy recorded the last days of these bands in the first half of the nineteenth century, when they still played in church and for all the local dances and celebrations. William Holloway remembered the village musicians:

> Constant at church, they lead the village quire,
> Where sacred music set the soul on fire;
> And well they knew to touch the breathing reed
> To gayer notes, which sprightly dances lead

The Bishop's notes on his visits to Dorset show that although Holy Communion was only celebrated three or four times a year, only a few people took it. At Pimperne, from 62 families (all Church of England) less than 25 took communion. This was a common pattern: church attendance but not taking communion.

Pluralism, (the holding of several parishes together by one person), was also common, with a lowly curate employed to conduct services. Absenteeism also occurred: at Buckhorn Weston in 1766 the Bishop noted that the rector does 'not reside constantly [i.e. live in his parish] and complains much of ill-health, tho he looks the picture of health itself'.

Other ministers were described as 'very wicked and drunken' (Gussage All Saints, 1735) or even 'a worthless fellow and much in debt' (West Parley 1766). But the Bishop also listed excellent ministers, like John Hutchins the historian, rector of Wareham, who attracted high numbers to communion services, or John Hubbock of Dorchester who was 'a worthy man and constantly resident'; and taught the Grammar School as well as preaching twice every Sunday. He also held services on Wednesdays and Saturdays, a rarity then.

The squireson, a man who was both squire and parson, certainly existed in the eighteenth century, and was often one of the more worldly ministers, but in total control of his parish since he was both secular and spiritual leader. The rector of Ibberton from 1775-1802 sounds a more reasonable mixture than the extremes the Bishop lists. 'He was a cheerful companion, and at all times acceptable in the social circles, among the lower class of people he not only theoretically taught the precepts of Christianity, but his heart and hand were

John Hutchins (1698-1773), rector of Wareham, and
the author of the huge *History and Antiquities of the
County of Dorset*, (published posthumously in 1774).
His work would have been lost in the great fire of
Wareham (1762) if his wife had not bravely gathered
up and saved the extensive manuscript and all his
notes. The rectory was reduced to ashes.

ever ready to relieve the necessitous to the utmost of his ability.'
Hutchins quotes his shrewd 'answer to the Bishop of the diocese at
Bath about residence: when the Bishop asked how many of the
incumbents came to Bath? he asked, how many more in proportion
of the bishops?'

Other rectors were scholars, some studying the archaeology,
history, natural history of their areas. John Hutchins, rector of
Wareham, was the most important of these, producing his great
two-volume *History of Dorset* in 1774. Others studied wider matters.

The Unitarian Chapel at Bridport was built in 1794, and still has most of its original fittings. The side galleries, columns and pews are much the same as those used in contemporary churches, but in the chapel the pulpit is placed where the altar would be in a church.

An obituary of the Rev Giles Templeman, vicar of Wimborne St Giles in the mid eighteenth century, stated: 'The time which others spent in visiting, in trifling reading, or in the amusement of the field [hunting etc.] he employed in an attentive perusal of the classical writings of the ancients or of the authors more immediately connected with his profession'. The obituarist also emphasised Templeman's 'strict attention to the duties of his office', indicating that a man could be both a scholar and a good parish priest.

The Bishop's notes for Dorset make clear that Non-conformity was strong in the county. Despite the good works of John Hutchins, half the families in Wareham were Presbyterian, and at Bridport in 1766 from the 433 families which inhabited the town, 130 were Non-conformists. 56 were Presbyterian, 49 Independent, 11 Anabaptists and 14 Quakers. There were also four Catholic families who worshipped at Chideock. Dorset had a much higher proportion of Nonconformists than the country as a whole. Because they were divided into many sects, there were many small chapels, which ranged from cottages adapted for worship to small classical buildings especially constructed for the purpose.

Catholicism was almost illegal for much of the eighteenth century. Because the Welds, one of Dorset's land-owning families was Catholic, the religion survived in small pockets in the county. Disapproval of the religion was not universal, but could be vehement. Hutchins (1774) baldly stated that 'some have expressed a dislike that any mention should be made of the medieval monasteries of the county in this history, as if the superstitious rites of former ages had penetrated into and infected the very walls.' Catholicism is seen as an infection, and he also refers to the corruptions of the church of Rome.

ROADS, TRAVEL AND INNS

At the beginning of the eighteenth century, travel in the county was difficult. Most roads were in a bad condition, as they had been for centuries. Parishes were responsible for their own roads, and were supposed to repair them, but little was done. From the middle of the century things improved because main routes were privatised. Turnpike Trust companies took over specific roads by Act of Parliament, repaired them (and often re-routed parts), and charged tolls to anyone using that road. They placed gates across the road, with toll-houses for the gate-keepers who took the money.

The first Dorset turnpike was the Shaftesbury and Sherborne of 1752, and in the next twenty years every major route in the county was taken over by Turnpike Trusts. Improvements in road-building methods (surfacing, drainage etc.) combined with the efforts of the Turnpike Trusts produced a good network of major roads all over the county. Many bridges were rebuilt, and signposts and mileposts were provided, the first in Dorset since Roman times.

The traffic on these roads consisted of carriages for passengers, wagons for goods, and wagons or carts which were used locally by farmers. Men often travelled on horseback, but women only rarely. Transport for the mass of the people was the same as it had been since earliest times - they walked.

The wagons for goods were large, heavy vehicles which needed a team of eight horses to drag them and moved at less than walking pace, usually only two miles an hour. Sea transport for goods was much cheaper and easier, but less reliable because shipping depended on the wind. Regular wagon services were run on several routes through Dorset.

Wagons did take the occasional passenger, but the more expensive stage-coaches were much quicker. These public coaches had been established at the end of the seventeenth century, running regular

Fordington, on the outskirts of Dorchester in the 1770s, with a coach and six using the new road across the watermeadows made possible by the construction of Grey's Bridge in 1748.

services on fixed routes. The stage-coaches were faster than any earlier public transport and impressed contemporaries, but it took two and a half days to reach Dorchester from London. The coaches changed horses regularly, and stopped at inns for the nights. In 1772 it cost £1.25p to travel from London to Blandford by coach, and £1.60p to Bridport. These prices were enormous: a labourer's weekly wage was only about 8s or 9s at most. The regularity of the services (the Blandford coach left London on Tuesdays and Thursdays; the Bridport coach Mondays and Thursdays) was a great improvement, but since one coach could only carry about fifteen passengers the services were hardly mass transport.

The Black Bear at Wareham, a typical late eighteenth century town coaching inn, with a large figure of a bear on the projecting porch to show visitors where to come.

Local traffic on the roads included farm wagons taking produce to market, privately owned coaches and smaller horse-drawn vehicles belonging to the gentry. Pack horses (or sometimes donkeys) were still used to transport goods, but they didn't use the roads. They simply took the most direct route on paths across country.

Travelling by ship was a cheaper alternative for passengers to

Hauling in mackerel off Chesil Beach in 1791. Horses with
panniers wait to take the catch inland to sell it.

London or other ports, but the length of time the journey took
depended on the wind. No service was run especially for longer
distance passengers: cargoes were the main trade and passengers an
extra. Smaller boats ran along the coast. In March 1759 the ferry
boat which ran between Poole and Ower (on the other side of Poole
Harbour) ran aground in bad weather, and of the 19 people on
board, only six were saved. The list of passengers gives a snapshot of
those travelling back from Poole market - a steward to one of the
local landowners, five farmers, one butcher, one miller, a marble
worker, a stocking knitter, two shoemakers, a sailor and one servant.
No occupations are given for the four women in the boat. All were
returning to Purbeck, probably to Corfe since Ower was a very small
settlement.

Whilst travelling on horseback from London to Weymouth in the
autumn of 1782 John Byng complained, 'Travelling alone with a
taper purse [i.e. little money] affords inconvenience and misery; and
a groom is absolutely necessary for your horses welfare.' He had
great difficulty in getting decent service from the inns he stayed at
because he had no luggage and no servant. The distance he travelled
each day had to be calculated around the capacity of his horse -
unlike the stage-coaches he was only using one horse the whole
way. Beds were generally bad - dirty blankets at Winchester, not
more 'than fiftey feathers in the bolster and pillow, or double that

A coach arriving at the King's Arms, Dorchester, in the late eighteenth century.

Early eighteenth century trade card from the White Hart, Dorchester
advertising 'Neat Post Coach & Chaises with able Horses'. Inns hired out
carriages as well as horses, acting as a combination of hotel, pub and garage.

number in the feather-bed' at Ringwood. When he finally arrived at Weymouth, his first need was to stable the horse at one of the hotels. He visited the horse daily, rode him sometimes, and had to take him to be shod.

On leaving Weymouth, he tried to dine at a roadside alehouse, but could not because there was no man to take care of his horse. Alehouses were local public houses, not equipped like inns to deal with the traveller and his horse. The Woodyates Inn, right in the north of the county put him into a rage; 'I look upon an inn, as the seat of all roguery, profaness, and debauchery; and sicken of them every day, by hearing nothing but oaths, and abuse of each other, and brutality to horses.' He blamed 'The universal fashion to go post [i.e. to travel by public coach]; the higher that is taxed the better, and then good road houses may again be had, and good stabling too.' Byng thought the old days were better: transport only got worse even in the eighteenth century.

INDUSTRIES

Georgian Dorset had a surprising number of industries large enough to send materials or even finished goods far afield.

Quarrying for stone was already an ancient industry in Purbeck, and Portland's quarries had expanded enormously from the 1660s, after Sir Christopher Wren chose it for the new St Paul's Cathedral. Appreciation of the superlative white stone, so suited to classical architecture, grew.

In 1793 John Claridge surveyed Dorset's industries, noting that the whole Isle of Portland seemed to be 'one intire mass of the most beautiful stone, chiefly used in the metropolis and elsewhere for the most superb buildings, and universally admired for its close texture and durability, surpassing any other'. The stone was sold in large rough blocks, and he estimated that 30 to 40 thousand tons were shipped off the island each year.

The quarries in Purbeck were underground mines, and differed from Portland also in that much of the stone was shaped into finished products before being shipped. Claridge thought it 'excellent stone for walling, floors, steps, and in particular for foot pavements in towns, for tomb-stones, troughs, and feet and caps for rick staddles'. The mushroom-like staddle stones (supports for barns or corn ricks) cost 36s (£1.80p) for a set of nine at Swanage, but carriage would have made them much more expensive elsewhere. Fifty thousand tons of Purbeck stone were being shipped annually from Swanage.

Clay quarrying was another expanding industry. Ball clay for making tobacco pipes had been quarried in the heathlands south of Poole Harbour from the seventeenth century. From the 1760s it was also used by Josiah Wedgewood for his fine earthenware (creamware), and production soared. In 1793 Claridge noted that about eleven thousand tons were shipped each year, and about 100 men were employed digging the clay.

A wooden barn on staddle stones, like those made in Purbeck. The stone supports kept the whole building up out of the damp, and helped to prevent rats entering the building. The staddle stones were usually used to support granaries which are particularly vulnerable to rats and mice. Wimborne Minster is in the background. Painted by Rev. J. Rackett in 1780.

Probably the most important manufacturing industry was the long-established production of ropes, sails, and nets at Bridport and Beaminster. Sailcloth was made all over west Dorset and south Somerset. Claridge though this manufactory a great support for poor people because the spinning of the flax and hemp into twine was handwork, needing a great many people.

Button making was a new industry for Georgian Dorset, and again employed many out-workers. In 1796 Hutchins records the industry at Affpuddle 'as a sort of small manufacture which [the women] are more generally getting into now, the making of shirt buttons, at which an expert hand can earn 3s 6d a week', whereas women working in the fields only earnt 5d a day.

A small amount of cloth-manufacturing continued in the county,

but most of the products were of poor quality and little value. A coarse white woollen cloth called swanskin was made at Shaftesbury and Sturminster Newton, and other types elsewhere in the county. Twisting silk into skeins was an important industry at Sherborne, and stockings were knitted around Wimborne.

Blocks of Portland stone near Rufus Castle in about 1790. The men may be quarry masters, or merchants who have come to buy the stone. Their meal is set out on one block. Portland stone was exported in large blocks like these, rather than 'being sent off Portland as finished goods.' In the late 18th century it usually cost 10s a ton to ship Portland stone to London.

THE PEOPLE

The idea that pre-industrial society was static, with everyone living in the same village their ancestors had inhabited, with son following father in a continuous series at the same trade, is such a deeply held folk myth that it must fulfil some need in modern people. It is tied up with the whole idea of an earlier, simpler life and society, when work was physical, hard and rewarding, society stratified and secure, and somehow everything was more real and satisfying, despite the small compass most lives were restricted to.

In fact, everywhere that the eighteenth century population has been studied, it has been found to be very much more mobile than the stereotype. Typically at least half the inhabitants of a village were not born there, and all through the eighteenth century many people were leaving the land altogether and moving to the towns, or more likely to London.

The greatest difficulty in imagining earlier times is accepting that they were very stratified societies. People then saw the world as a pyramid of rank, with the aristocracy at the top and the begging vagabond at the bottom. Every one knew their place, and it was possible to see immediately what class someone was by their dress. Society was held together by the rights and duties of the different ranks. The rich had a duty to support the poor; servants the duty to be loyal and industrious.

A memorial stone erected at Over Compton near Sherborne, by the owner of the big house, to Henry Dyte who died in 1810 embodies some of these duties:

'He was workman and bailiff to the family of the Goddens here more than sixty years, in whose service he was uniformly most industrious, most honest, most faithful, most obstinately just, and his integrity was incorruptible. He is now gone to receive that reward which the Almighty in his mercy grants to those who discharge their

The superb memorial of 1775 to the wife of Lord Milton of Milton Abbas, the very top of Dorset society. Lord Milton, who lies beside her, rebuilt Milton Abbas house and the new village.

duties here conscientiously. Reader! if in an humble situation, go and imitate his conduct, for exceed it you cannot.' The certainty of the Goddens that they can declare what God is doing strikes modern eyes oddly.

Women were valued as wives and mothers: the inscription on Mary Place's memorial at Marnhull of 1741 is typical: 'a pattern of piety, and pure example of all the domestic and conjugal virtues as a wife, a mother, and mistress of a family. It was her principal care to observe the will, and contribute to the ease and happiness of her husband.'

Her duties as the mistress of a family were distinct from those of wife and mother: the word family in the eighteenth century extended to mean the household, including all the servants and often other relatives too. To be a good master or mistress meant to care for all the household both physically and morally. A master was responsible for the behaviour of the extended family: beggars and vagabonds were often called masterless men, because there was no-one to answer for them. William Holloway's poem 'The Peasant's Fate' recalls the old-time hospitality and simplicity of the master and mistress of the largest village household:

> *The worthy* Squire *will be remember'd long,*
> *The theme and pride of every cottage song,*
> *His* Lady *too . . . the patroness and friend*
> *Of all whom merit, worth, or want commend;*
> *Whose heart benevolent, and lib'ral mind,*
> *Nor prejudice nor narrow views confin'd.*
> *With grateful joy the widow heard her voice,*
> *Which bade e'en pale Infirmity rejoice,*
> *While virtuous orphans, objects of her care,*
> *Translated to her household, flourish'd fair.*
> *Their well-known mansion, on the green hill's side,*
> *O'erlook'd the village with a decent pride;*
> *But not with pompous arrogance deterr'd*
> *The meanest wretch, that there his suit preferr'd*

PEOPLE ON THE LAND

It has been estimated that the population of Dorset in 1750 was about 90,000. By the time of the first proper census in 1801 it had risen to 115,000. Less than one-third of these people lived in towns in 1801, and even so some of the town-dwellers were agriculturists. At the beginning of the eighteenth century the towns were still smaller: most of Dorset depended directly on farming.

The Georgian countryside was seen as a lost paradise of stability by the Victorians, who imagined it to have been populated by rosy-cheeked milkmaids and solid yeoman farmers, who all knew their lowly place in the hierarchy and were happy with it.

Despite the tendency to romance earlier agriculture, the eighteenth century was a better time for those at the bottom of the heap. At the beginning of the period there were many more small farmers, but gradually farms were being amalgamated and becoming much larger. Enclosure (either of the old medieval open fields, or of new lands) also tended to favour the larger landowner. William Barnes lamented the continuing change:

> *Then ten good dearies [dairies] were a-ved*
> *Along that water's winden bed,*
> *An in the lewth o' hills and wood*
> *A half a score farm-housen stood:*
> *But now, - count all o'm how you would,*
> *So many less do hold the land, -*
> *You'd vind but vive that still do stand,*
> *A-comen down vrom gramfer's.*

The dairies, in typical Dorset fashion, were in addition to the farmhouses because they were run separately.

Certainly the eighteenth century had more in common with earlier society than the nineteenth century. More labourers lived in the farmer's house, and had better food because of it. There were more small farmers, many of whom also had a trade. But it was not the paradise that hindsight imagined.

A survey of the large village of Bere Regis in 1776 shows that 26 of the 46 tenants held less than 30 acres. Seven of the fourteen tradesmen in Bere also held land, working as part-time farmers. Gradually plots were amalgamated, new ground broken for arable and the great variety of holdings was replaced by a few large farms. The diversity of the eighteenth century, with land-holdings varying from 20 acres or less to farms of more than 300 acres, was destroyed.

The decline in the number of farmers is clearly shown by the number of ratepayers, as usually only occupiers of land paid rates. At Winterborne Monkton eighteen people paid in 1730, with the rates varying from 4d to 1s 6d. The numbers gradually declined (eleven in 1760, eight in 1780, five in 1790) until in 1800 there are only two - the parson and one large farmer.

The rector of Marnhull recorded his recollections of the parish in the 1760s, when 'the men were remarkable for being badly made about the legs, knock knees, and spindle shanks', which he blamed on 'the badness of the roads and wetness of the soil at that time, and

Traditional farmyards were composed of a clutter of buildings of many dates. This example from Winfrith gives a good idea of the variety, with an open-fronted cart shed and a big barn made out of an earlier building.

the boys wearing shoes so heavily shod with iron that they could with difficulty drag them along . . . as [the men] were great cudgel-players, it was a common saying, that it was a hard matter to break a Marnhull man's *head*, but a trifling stroke would break his *leg*.' The rector showed intense local pride, and a surprising acceptance of what seems to us a harsh sport. The village was also 'much given to agues; but industry and necessity have delivered us from that scourge; industry by draining our lands . . . and necessity by making the proprietors of the lands cut down all the timber trees and woods, and letting in a free current of air': trees were regarded as unhealthy in the eighteenth century: one of Weymouth's boasts was that the resort did not have any.

All this was improvement, and by 1815, when the rector was writing, the village was full of 'many stout, handsome well-grown men', but he did complain of the lack of houses 'owing to the ruinous practice of letting large farms . . . detrimental to the

The smaller and less well-built cottages have rarely survived. This single storey thatched cottage at Corfe Castle dates from the early 18th century: it had three rooms downstairs and a little stair leading to the attic in the roof.

community at large, as 300 acres let to three different tenants will raise and produce more commodities for the market than 300 acres let to one man.' The population had increased, but the number of houses had decreased. The rector of Hawkchurch (then in Dorset) had a similar complaint. In the mid eighteenth century 'ten farmers lived independently, and brought up their families with comfort, credit and respectability, on the very lands' now occupied by one large farmer.

In 1741 Bere Regis had built a parish poor house. Many Dorset parishes constructed or took over cottages for the poor at about this time, because the numbers of paupers were increasing.

The poor came from the class of landless labourers, who were employed by the larger farmers. Poor relief was administered by the parish, who collected a poor rate, and distributed it to those who needed it. Usually small amounts of money were given each week to enable the paupers to maintain themselves in their own cottages. This was called outdoor relief. The parish paid out in times of sickness, unemployment, childbirth, death and madness. The relief was often in kind. The Radipole accounts for 1764 show Abraham Scriven being supplied with three shirts, two new pairs of 'shoos', breeches, and even having the shoes mended. Three people's house rent was paid for them.

All this, along with four more pairs of shoes, two sheets, a new coat and waistcoat, another pair of breeches and a hat, were paid for by 'one years hire of Abraham Scriven to Farmer Kibber at 18d a week which the farmer took him on for the parish cloathing him.' More usually the money came from the parish poor rate. Sometimes the parish paid for work to be done for the public good. In 1786 Stephen Isles was paid 8d a day for 12 days work flattening ant hills on the common to improve the communal grazing.

The type and amount of payment made varied from parish to parish, but in many places those in receipt of relief had to wear a parish badge to show their shameful pauper status. Settlement was the major problem with this system. In order to be paid, a person had to have settlement in the parish, i.e. be able to prove that they belonged there. If they did not, they were returned to their native parish if they became ill or a pauper. Parishes wanted to limit their responsibilities,

A thatched privy of 1790, sketched by
Hieronymus Grimm at Abbotsbury.

so only those born there, or those who could prove long residence,
obtained settlement. Parishes could evict anyone who moved in if
they even suspected they might at some time need paying relief.

The surviving list of the food given at Beaminster workhouse in
1774 gives a good idea of the minimum diet. Milk broth and oatmeal
was the usual breakfast and supper, varied occasionally by pease
broth and oatmeal for supper, or bread for breakfast. Four days a
week lunch was simply bread, but on Fridays it was bacon and
vegetables, on Sundays bacon or beef with vegetables, and Tuesdays
bacon and peas. Vegetables (including the peas) only came to 3 oz a
week, but the bread per week was 96 oz. A monotonous and seem-
ingly rather unhealthy diet.

It used to be assumed that enclosure was the cause of the
impoverishment of many labourers, but it is now believed that simple

pressure caused by increasing population was the main reason, with the growing size of farms a subsidiary cause.

In the early eighteenth century there was far more shading from one class to another, with the small farmer or tradesman shading down to the landless labourer, and up to the bigger farmers. Later in the century it was much more difficult for a labourer to become a farmer because the smaller land-holdings had ceased to exist. Arthur Young in his *Tour* of 1771 did meet one man who had succeeded in becoming a farmer. William White rose 'from being a day labourer to a little farmer'. Somehow he saved £200 in twenty years; 'an instance of frugality and sobriety which is much to his honour among so many poor neighbours, whose conduct is the very reverse' according to Young. (How he did this, when wages for a day labourer were only about £15 a year is not revealed). He rented boggy land, and turned it into water-meadow, starting with only two acres and extending to 87, half of it arable. Young estimated that the farmer's leasehold, stock etc., was now worth £1150, and emphasised that many labourers could do the same if they had but the resolution. Young's detailed description of William White in fact shows how rare he was. All of the other farmers Young describes were on a much larger scale, better placed to exploit new methods and crops.

William Holloway was born in West Dorset in 1761, the younger son of a small yeoman farmer. His poetry often explored the countryside of his youth, and he had no doubt who was to blame for the impoverishment of labourers and small farmers, described in his long poem 'The Peasant's Fate' (1802):

> *For, lo a venal band*
> *On Nature's bounty lay the griping hand,*
> *Wrest from the poor the partimonal cot,*
> *His paddock add to their superfluous lot,*
> *Meanly dependent, bid him seek his bread,*
> *While, Timur-like, their vassal down they tread,*
> *Frustrate the scheme wise Providence has plann d,*
> *And half depopulate their native land.*

Holloway's introduction makes clear that it is the large farmer and his quest for luxurious living which has ruined the poor peasant.

Shallow bay windows were added to this house in Sturminster Newton in the early eighteenth century when it became a shop.

Farmers were becoming much more middle class during the eighteenth century. Earlier, they and their sons had worked the land alongside their hired hands, and the farmer's wife and daughters had milked the cows and made the butter and cheese. By the end of the century it was only the exceptional farmer or his children who worked in field or dairy.

VILLAGE TRADESMEN

The population of a Georgian village consisted mostly of farmers and labourers, but there were also tradesmen. Some of these were also small farmers. Each village needed a mill to grind wheat into flour, a blacksmith to shoe the horses and mend implements and a builder for houses and barns. Larger villages had a greater variety of trades. A complete survey of Puddletown in 1724 shows that for a population of about 600 there were three millers and one maltster producing malt for brewing. An inn and an ale-house sold some of the beer. Seven men were in the building trade, including two thatchers. Four blacksmiths and three wheelwrights (making carts as well as the wheels) looked after transport, and a cooper made barrels. Three woolstaplers dealt with the raw wool, along with one weaver and a worsted comber who processed it. Five tailors and three shoemakers supplied clothes, and three barbers cut hair and shaved men. There were three or four shopkeepers, one butcher and two bakers. Three teachers kept schools, and there were twenty two servants. The most surprising trade is the man who was a clock-maker and gunsmith. Overall, Puddletown needed little from the outside world - from shoes and bread to clocks and cloth, Puddletown produced its own. The list of trades sounds much more like a town than a village.

RURAL HOLIDAYS

One of the losses most regretted by the Victorians was the series of seasonal celebrations and holidays which had punctuated the rural year. John Pennie writing in 1827, looked back to the mid-eighteenth century at Lulworth, romanticising his parent's and grandparent's memories of the past. He listed 'some of the amusements that many years ago used to give spirit, happiness, and content to the merry-hearted rustics ... all of which, from the innovating changes of manner and times, have now passed away'. On May-day 'the peasant maidens flocked early to the dewy fields, the gardens, and the woods, to gather sheaves of fresh-blown flowers to decorate the gaudy May-staff [or pole] which was the rendezvous of the young, the sportive,

Bere Marsh Mill, Shillingstone, a neat example of a Georgian
industrial building of plain brick, but with a decorative band under
the roof. It has since been demolished.

and the idle, and the meeting place of the aged and garrulous, who
held there every evening their general councils.' A dance was held
on May-day evening around the pole and many other dances were
regularly held in one of the huge barns.

The 5th of November was celebrated by a bonfire with 'guns firing,
bells ringing ... and flagons of ale at the expense of the parish.'
Lulworth burnt an effigy of the Pope along with one of Guy Fawkes
which seems tactless as the landowners were Catholic.

Pennie is particularly lyrical about the Harvest Home. 'The last
wagon loaded with nodding sheaves came from the field, covered
with boughs and garlands of flowers ... while the jovial shouts of
happy reapers resounded from grove to grove ... the harvest-feast
was spread for all the industrious poor, all the hardy peasantry on
the farm, young and old, on the loaded tables of the hospitable but
unostentatious farmer of those days.'

The end of sheep-shearing was also celebrated by a supper, 'but
such vulgar feastings cannot now be endured in the polite dwellings
of members belonging to the new school of husbandry.'

Pennie's romantic nostalgia paints far too perfect a world: all is flower-garlanded in his happy peasant past, where it never rains. However, he is right about the cycle of annual celebrations which had enriched this earlier world, and right also in that the farmers had joined with everyone else for these events.

Another rural holiday was the fair, for the buying and selling of goods and livestock. They were held annually, or sometimes more frequently, often far away from towns. Woodbury Hill near Bere Regis was the site of the most important Dorset fair, described by Hutchins in 1774 as attracting traders 'from Birmingham, Norwich, Exeter, Bristol, London, and other parts of England. Vast Quantities of hops, cloth, cheese, and almost all commodities, were sold here'. The fair lasted a week from September 18th, with wholesale trade only on the first day. Hutchins notes that the tolls had fallen by the 1770s to half that of the 1730s. Fairs were becoming less important as more shops opened in the towns, but they preserved an important role, partly because they were traditional meeting places, and offered amusements alongside the trading.

Towns also had their fairs, fixed to the farming year. At Dorchester there were four each year, recorded by the 1792 *Universal British Directory* as '12th February for cattle and all sorts of sheep; on Trinity Monday and July 5, for sheep, lambs and all sorts of cattle; and on 5th August for all sorts of sheep, cattle, wool and leather.' These were the main goods sold, but stalls offered many other goods. Markets and fairs both declined a little during the eighteenth century as direct sales of animals, butter, cheese etc. to London and other centres increased.

ELECTIONS

Parliamentary elections were the only elections in the eighteenth century. The Corporations which administered the towns were oligarchies - the members of the council themselves chose any new members needed.

There were two MPs to represent the county, and their elections were reasonably straightforward. It was in the eight boroughs that corrupt elections flourished. A tiny borough like Corfe Castle had two MPs as did Bridport, Dorchester, Lyme Regis, Poole, Shaftesbury, Wareham and Weymouth. Bribes were routinely issued to those

An alas difficult to illustrate but extremely rare cotton
handkerchief printed for the Dorchester election of 1790.
Francis Fane was elected, but he had little to do
with freedom or independence. The handkerchief was
probably presented to a voter, along with cash.

lucky enough to qualify as voters. A list of election expenses for Corfe in 1784 records matter-of-factly 'To 45 Voters at 13s each'. The total bill was £84, and included five Half Hogsheads of Beer on the Election Day (plus 2s 6d 'To Two persons to protect the Beer'), dinners for the voters and payments to the bell ringers. Election day was a holiday.

Beer and simple money bribes were enough in Corfe, elsewhere bribery with money went hand-in-hand with slightly more subtle offers of jobs or simple influence. At Poole in 1768 two voters wanted to be Mayor: one was assured that they would get it, the other had to be content with being made the officer for the Sun Fire Office. At least financial bribes were secure - promises of jobs were not always fulfilled. If a voter would not agree to vote for the right person, attempts might be made to drive him temporarily out of town, to prevent him voting. At Poole in 1768 one side was accused of locking one voter up, and the other managed to have a voter arrested for debt. One candidate's expenses in this 1768 election came to almost a thousand pounds. Voting was public, so it was easy for candidates to check that those they had bribed voted the right way.

Only some of the inhabitants in the towns had the right to vote, which depended on owning property. At Weymouth it was claimed that all free-holders had the right, but in other towns the numbers qualified to vote were very much smaller.

CHILDREN AND EDUCATION

For the lower classes, especially the children of rural labourers, there was little education in eighteenth century Dorset. If they were lucky, there was a local dame school which taught a little reading and needlework. Since the parents had to pay, many poorer families could not afford to send their children. Many of these dame schools only catered for very young children - 2-6 years. An honest keeper of such a school in Dorset admitted that they were mostly for keeping children out of mischief.

Most of the towns had ancient Grammar Schools intended to educate local boys free of charge, but by Georgian times most of these were charging fees too, and were educating the sons of the upper and middle classes from a wider area. These grammar- school educated boys were the only ones who would go on to Oxford or Cambridge, then the only universities.

When Dorset charities were listed in the early nineteenth century, there were 52 for education, and about 20 more helped with apprenticeships. Most of these were founded in the early eighteenth century or even earlier. The charity schools were almost always better than dame schools.

Elizabeth Ham, an upper middle class girl, first attended a small school in Dorchester in the late eighteenth century. She wrote in her memoirs, 'I have no great idea of what we did at Mrs Mason's besides learning a dozen words in a spelling book, reading once in the morning and once in the afternoon, and sitting the remainder of the time on the form sewing.' At another school in Weymouth, she remembered long hours spent 'with hot hands and creaking needle in a closed room, packed side by side on a long form with others as hot and sleepy as myself.' Girls' education included a great deal of needlework, and usually other accomplishments like music, dancing and drawing as well. Too much intellect in women was to be avoided, so girls' education was limited. Elizabeth Ham regretted her poor education, and looking back in later life realised that 'not one of the governesses it was my fate to be placed under knew as much education as could now be found in any mistress of any village charity school.'

In the late eighteenth century Sunday Schools were established, not as a kind of junior church, but for general education. A whole group were established in Purbeck by 1792, with 13 schools and over a thousand pupils. The national rules for the formation and regulation of Sunday Schools suggested that 'neither writing or arithmetic should be taught', but only reading, based on the Bible. 'The religious observance of the Sabbath, and the improvement of virtuous habits, being the great objects of the institution.' Surprisingly, children of all Protestant denominations were welcomed, not just those belonging to the Church of England. William Pitt, who founded the Purbeck group of schools, stated his aims: 'these schools extend religious knowledge among the ignorant [and] they instil into the lower classes of the community industry, decency, sobriety, and that respectful deportment towards superiors, which is perfectly consistent with true liberty and the pride of industrious independence.'

715 children attended the first annual meeting at Corfe, 'But a few months before, far the greater number of these children were in a state of total ignorance', but the improvement in reading, behaviour and manners was striking. Most of the children who attended Sunday School would have been at work all week.

The Sunday Schools were funded by the local gentry and clergy, and like most education for the lower classes emphasised 'respectful deportment to superiors', including those who funded and ran the schools. The Purbeck group was a brave attempt to bring at least some education to the children of labourers, but it was to be overtaken by wider measures in the nineteenth century.

Work was more important than education for most rural children. Families needed even the tiny wages boys could earn in the fields. Jobs for seven year olds included bird-scaring and minding grazing animals. Girls worked in the fields and dairies too. In the towns more boys (and some girls) were likely to be apprenticed to a trade.

A classical temple, built for ornament not pagan rites, at
Kingston Maurward. It dates from about 1780.

Interest in the past was becoming more scientific in the Georgian
period. Since the normal secondary education was firmly rooted in
Latin, Roman remains were particularly prized because they could be
related to the classics. Some Dorset monuments had been noted by
seventeenth century topographers, but Stukeley's *Itinarium Curiosum*
(1726) was a much more thorough survey. He published prospects
and plans of the amphitheatre at Dorchester, establishing that it was
Roman, and traced several Roman roads. He realised that the road
into Dorchester from the west was Roman, and complained that 'in
divers places they have mended it, where wore out, by a small slip of
chalk and flints, with a shameful and degenerate carelessness; so
that we may well pronounce the Romans worked with shovels, the
moderns with tea-spoons.'

Stukeley was particularly impressed with the tumuli on the hills
around Dorchester, and thought that 'for sight of barrows' the view
from Maiden Castle was 'not to be equalled in the world; for
they reach ten miles.' He was ahead of his time in appreciating

pre-Roman remains, and was appalled at the indifference to the prehistoric remains round Dorchester. The gentry of Dorset would soon catch up with his interest in antiquities, but he recorded some of the local labourers defending them even before his arrival. 'Some farmers were levelling another great barrow; but the people of Fordington rose in arms and prevented them.' Their objections probably had more to do with folk beliefs, or even opposition to enclosure, than to an interest in prehistory.

By the middle of the century, when Hutchins' great *History of Dorset* was being prepared, interest in all the past had grown. Medieval buildings were engraved for the book, along with Roman mosaics and finds. Plans of several prehistoric earthworks (Maiden Castle, Eggardon, Maumbury etc.) were published, but were still thought to be Roman.

In John O Keefe's play of 1793, *The London Hermit, or Rambles in Dorsetshire* (based on his stays at West Lulworth), his old-fashioned gentry character dislikes the emphasis on classical (and therefore foreign) display: 'Your modern gardens are art spoiling nature; fixing up a stone woman where one expects to find a rosy girl of health, flesh, and blood: if we must have statues, instead of importing ancient heather gods into English meadows, why not encourage British arts to celebrate British heroes?'

THE GEORGIAN LEGACY

Georgian Dorset has left many legacies to the present-day county, but its landscape has been much altered. Two hundred years of improvements in farming have led to the enclosure and ploughing-up of much of the characteristic chalk downlands, and little remains of the vast heathlands. Only in the clay vales does the farming remain similar, still being based on cattle. Machinery has replaced the armies of Georgian labourers, leaving the countryside a much lonelier place, and the villages inhabited by people who do not work on the land. Farmyards have been transformed by Victorian and modern buildings suitable for changed farming methods.

Most villages and towns have also been changed, with the addition of many more elaborate buildings. Almost every settlement has grown considerably, and in some places (like Poole) there has been wholesale demolition of the Georgian. Happily, the rigid hierarchy of Georgian society has finally gone, leaving only a residual snobbishness. Even the smallest hamlet is now part of the wider world, and local markets for local produces are no more.

Our large inheritance of Georgian buildings is nowadays much appreciated. We no longer wish to make properly medieval the few Georgian churches (as the Victorians did on the grounds that classical buildings were somehow not Christian). Most of the Georgian pews were lost to Victorian reformers, but the surviving Georgian church fittings are prized, as is Georgian furniture, even the simpler type made for farmers.

Dorset's Georgian legacy ranges from humble thatched cottages to huge mansions like Milton Abbas. Every town and village has plain, handsome brick or stone Georgian houses, but two towns are still largely of the period. Weymouth is full of Georgian terraces, and Blandford is such a perfectly preserved Georgian town that it has been made a World Heritage site.

FURTHER READING

Many quotations are taken from John Hutchins *History and Antiquities of the County of Dorset*, published in two volumes in 1774. The second edition, altered and augmented by several other people was issued in four volumes (1796-1815). All the memorial inscriptions, the Marnhull rector's description of his parish, the description of Hawkchurch, and of the Purbeck Sunday schools, come from this second edition. By normal convention, the second edition is called Hutchins if mentioned in the text, despite being written by other people.

Information on the poorhouses is taken from *The Administration of the Poor Laws in Dorset 1760-1834*, With Special Reference to Agrarian Distress (1967) by George A. Body (unpublished thesis: copy in Dorset County Library). Details of Bere Regis and its farming are from *Bound to the Soil: A Social History of Dorset* (1968) by Barbara Kerr (chapter six). The Puddletown Survey of 1724 is published in *Puddletown - House Street and Family* (1988) by C. L. Sinclair Williams. In the *Diary and Letters of Madame D'Arbley* (Fanny Burney) vol.V (1905) deals with Dorset. The details of the Bishop's surveys of Dorset are from 'Bishop Secker's Diocesan Survey' by J.H. Bettey in *Proceedings of the Dorset Natural History and Archaeological Society* volume 95. The Poole election material of 1768 comes from an article by Barbara Kerr in the same journal, vol. 89. The Corfe election expenses bill was published in *Somerset and Dorset Notes and Queries* vol. 7, p.65. The 1759 Poole ferry disaster is in the same journal, vol.8, 27-28. The Rev. Richard Paget's notes on Dorset are in the same journal vol.32, 787-790. The description of smugglers at Christchurch is quoted in *Smuggling in Hampshire & Dorset 1700-1850* (1983) by Geoffrey Morley (p.88). The census material is from the *Victoria County History - Dorset, vol. 2*.

Other books quoted are: *The Torrington Diaries* (1934) by Hon. John Byng; *Memoirs of Richard Cumberland* vol.i (1807); *Passages from the diaries of Mrs Philip Lybbe Powys* (1899) edited by Emily J. Climenson; *A Tour through the whole Island of Great Britain* (1726) by Daniel Defoe; *General View of the Agriculture of the County of Dorset* (1793) by John Claridge; *Elizabeth Ham by Herself* (1944); *Observations of the Western Counties* (1797) by William Maton; *The Tale of a Modern Genius, or, The Miseries of Parnassus* (1827) by John Pennie; *The Travels through England of Dr Richard Pococke* (1889) The Camden Society.

ACKNOWLEDGEMENTS

I am grateful to Christopher Chaplin and Marion Makinson for reading drafts of this book, and for their comments; to Dr Joe Bettey for reading the final version and for his comments; to Sheena Pearce for word-processing it all; and to the Dorset County Library (Reading and Reference) for all their help.

Most of the illustrations in this book came from the Dovecote Press collection, but I am grateful to the following for allowing the inclusion of illustrations in their possession or for which they hold the copyright. The British Library – Crown Copyright: pages 56, 57, 65: Country Life: frontispiece, page 13: Dorset County Library: pages 9, 55: Dorset County Museum: pages 15 (top), 40, 52, 71: Royal Commission Historical Monuments (England), © Crown Copyright: copyright page, pages 14, 15 (bottom), 27, 28 (both), 37, 39, 42, 46, 62 (both), 67, 75.

The

DISCOVER DORSET

Series of Books

A series of paperback books providing informative illustrated
introductions to Dorset's history, culture and way of life.
The following titles have so far been published.

All the books about Dorset published by The Dovecote Press
are available in bookshops throughout the county,
or in case of difficulty direct from the publishers.
The Dovecote Press Ltd, Stanbridge,
Wimborne, Dorset BH21 4JD
Tel: 01258 840549.